Lemurs

By Christopher Butz

Raintree

ANIMALS OF THE RAINFOREST

www.raintreepublishers.co.uk
Visit our website to find out more information about Raintree books.

To order:
- ☎ Phone 44 (0) 1865 888112
- 📄 Send a fax to 44 (0) 1865 314091
- 💻 Visit the Raintree Bookshop at www.raintreepublishers.co.uk to browse our catalogue and order online.

First published in Great Britain by Raintree Publishers, Halley Court, Jordan Hill, Oxford, OX2 8EJ, part of Harcourt Education.
Raintree is a registered trademark of Harcourt Education Ltd.

Originated by Dot Gradations Ltd
Printed and bound in Hong Kong and China by South China

ISBN 1 844 21094 4
07 06 05 04 03
10 9 8 7 6 5 4 3 2 1

British Library Cataloguing in Publication Data
Butz, Christopher
Lemurs - (Animals of the rainforest)
1. Lemurs - Juvenile literature
2. Rain forest ecology - Juvenile literature
I.Title 599.8'3
A catalogue for this book is available from the British Library.

Acknowledgements
The publishers would like to thank the following for permission to reproduce photographs:
NHPA, p. **5, 27**; all other photos courtesy of David Haring, Duke Primate Center.

Cover photograph by Wildlife Conservation Society/Dennis De Mello.

Every effort has been made to contact copyright holders of any material reproduced in this book. Any omissions will be rectified in subsequent printings if notice is given to the publishers.

Contents

Any words appearing in the text in bold, **like this**, are explained in the Glossary.

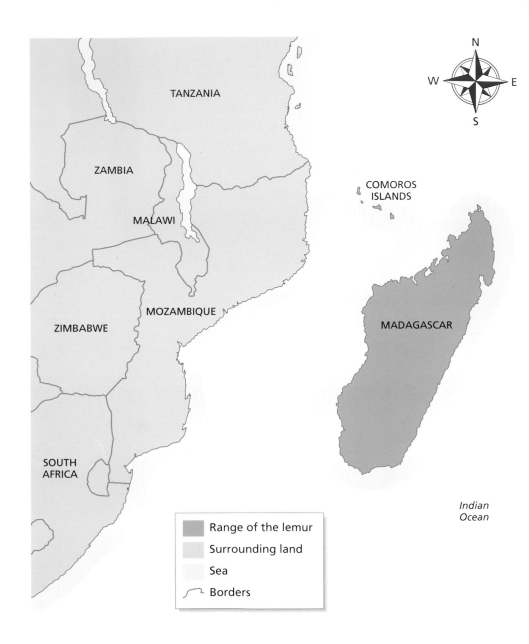

TANZANIA

ZAMBIA

MALAWI

ZIMBABWE

MOZAMBIQUE

SOUTH
AFRICA

COMOROS
ISLANDS

MADAGASCAR

N
W   E
S

Indian
Ocean

▆	Range of the lemur
▆	Surrounding land
▆	Sea
⌐⌐	Borders

A quick look at lemurs

What do lemurs look like?
Lemurs have furry, monkey-like bodies with long tails. They have fox-like faces. They also have large, unblinking eyes that are easy to see in the dark.

Where do lemurs live?
Almost all lemurs live on the island of Madagascar, which is off the south-east coast of Africa. It is the fourth largest island in the world. Some lemurs live on the Comoros Islands, which are between Madagascar and Africa.

What do lemurs eat?
Lemurs eat mainly fruit, flowers and leaves. Some eat insects and birds' eggs. Lemurs may lick the dew off leaves when they are thirsty, but most just drink water from rivers or streams.

This golden-crowned sifaka lemur is hanging from a branch in the rainforest.

Lemurs in the rainforest

Lemurs are monkey-like mammals with long tails. A mammal is a **warm-blooded** animal with a backbone. Female mammals give birth to mature young and feed them milk from their bodies. Warm-blooded animals have a body temperature that stays the same, no matter what the temperature is outside.

Lemurs are members of the **primate** order. An order is a group of animals that have many things in common. Primates are mammals that have a large brain and hands that can grasp and hold objects. Apes and monkeys are also primates. Unlike flat-faced monkeys, lemurs have long, fox-like, wet noses.

Lemurs' scientific name is Lemuroidea. It comes from a French word that means ghosts.

 These red-fronted lemurs are resting on the floor of the rainforest.

Where do lemurs live?

Most wild lemurs live on Madagascar, a large island in the Indian Ocean off the south-east coast of Africa. Two kinds of lemurs live on the Comoros Islands. These islands are between Madagascar and Africa. Lemurs can live in dry, flat places or in wet forests.

Most lemurs live in rainforests. A rainforest is a warm place where many different trees and plants grow close together, and a lot of rain falls. These lemurs are **arboreal** animals. Arboreal means living in the trees. Lemurs make their homes high in leafy tree branches. In a rainforest, the highest area of thick leaves and branches above the ground is called the **canopy**.

Lemurs are very good climbers and jumpers. Some lemurs spend almost all of their time in the trees. They eat and sleep in the canopy. At times, they climb down to drink water. Then they climb back into the treetops.

Some lemurs live alone. But most lemurs are social animals. Social animals are friendly to each other and live in groups. A lemur group may have from two to thirty lemurs of different ages and sexes in it. A group eats and sleeps together. Each group has its own area, which is called a home range. An animal lives and hunts in its home range.

Sometimes two groups of lemurs want to live in the same place. When this happens, the lemurs will fight each other. Sometimes ring-tailed lemurs will stink fight. To do this, males release scents from their bodies. They rub the scents on their tails. Then, they wave their stinky tails at the male lemurs from the other group until they run away.

What do lemurs look like?

All lemurs are covered with fur. The colour of the fur depends on the kind of lemur. Lemurs can be brown, black, white, grey or red. Some have colourful markings, like stripes, on their bodies or tails. Other lemurs have a growth of long hair around their heads. This growth of hair is called a ruff. It looks like a small lion's mane.

All lemurs, except the indri lemur, have a long, furry tail. Lemurs use their tails to help them balance as they move around. Some lemurs also use their tails to keep warm. They wrap them around their bellies on chilly days.

A lemur has five toes and five fingers. A nail grows on the end of each finger and toe, except the second toe of each foot. This second toe has a special claw called a **grooming** claw. The lemur uses this long claw to scratch and clean its fur. The aye-aye lemur has a long bony middle finger. It uses these fingers to probe inside tree bark to find insects to eat.

▲ You can see the ruff of hair around this
black-and-white ruffed lemur's face.

A lemur's head looks more like a fox's than a
monkey's. Monkeys have flat faces. But like
foxes, lemurs have wet noses on snouts that stick
out of their faces. Lemurs also have whiskers.

A lemur has large eyes that face forwards. Its
eyes work together to help it focus, which is
called **binocular vision**. Binocular vision helps the
lemur to tell how far away things are.

▲ This grey bamboo lemur is eating bamboo from a bamboo tree in which it lives.

Lemurs never blink their eyes because they do not have eyelids. Instead, a thin, clear covering protects the eyes and keeps them wet.

Kinds of lemurs

There are 36 known **species** of lemur. A species is a group of animals or plants that share common features and are closely related to each other.

Different kinds of lemur are different sizes. The tiniest lemur is the pygmy mouse lemur. It weighs only 30 grams, which is about as much as five sheets of paper. The largest lemurs are Madagascan indri lemurs. Their bodies are up to 70 centimetres long, with black and white markings.

Some lemur species are named after their markings. The ring-tailed lemur has black rings around its tail. Crowned lemurs have orange markings on their heads that look like crowns.

Some species of lemur are named after their colours. The red ruffed lemur has a reddish coat with a ruff of hair around its head. The black-and-white ruffed lemur has black and white fur and a ruff around its head. The blue-eyed lemur has bright blue eyes. Brown lemurs have brown fur.

Some lemurs are named after the trees in which they live. Bamboo lemurs live in **bamboo** trees. Grey bamboo lemurs have grey fur.

Lemur species mostly behave in the same way, but there are some differences. Larger species live in groups of up to 25 and are active during the day. Smaller species usually live alone or in small groups of two to eight. They sleep during the day and are **nocturnal** (active at night).

This mongoose lemur is eating the pollen from a flower.

What lemurs eat

Lemurs are **omnivores**. Omnivores are animals that eat both plants and other animals. Lemurs eat mainly plants, such as leaves, nuts, bark, flowers and fruit. Some species may eat insects. A few lemurs will also eat birds' eggs and chicks.

Different lemur species eat some foods more often than others. Nectar is a common food of black-and-white ruffed lemurs and red ruffed lemurs. Nectar is sweet liquid that flowers make. Some lemurs eat pollen. Pollen is a powdery material that plants make so new plants can grow. Other lemurs like the bark, pods and sap of the kily tree.

The aye-aye, a very unusual type of lemur, eats different food from most other lemurs. Along with fruit and nuts, it eats grubs and insects that live inside trees.

▲ This ring-tailed lemur is eating a flower growing in the rainforest canopy.

Finding and eating food

To find food, lemurs spend a lot of time travelling around their home ranges. Lemurs have a very good sense of smell. Most plants give off a scent. Although people cannot always smell plants, lemurs can find fruit and trees with their noses.

A few lemurs sometimes leave their main group to search for food. They use cries and calls to let other lemurs know where they are. They also call out to let other lemurs know if they have found food.

Unlike other primate groups, lemur groups are dominated mainly by the females. Dominate means to have the most power. Females usually lead the groups that search for food. They also get to eat the best food. They will take any food they want away from males.

There are two seasons in the rainforest – a rainy season and a dry season. During the October to April rainy season, a lot of rain falls. Many plants grow leaves, flowers and fruits. In these months, lemurs can easily find food to eat. They eat extra food during the rainy season. The bodies of some lemur species turn the extra food into fat. The fat is stored in their bodies. Mouse and dwarf lemurs store fat in their tails.

During the May to September dry season, little rain falls. In these months, it is difficult to find food. Dwarf and mouse lemurs then live off their stored fat. Other lemur species may eat food they would not usually eat, such as tree bark.

This red ruffed female is looking after her young lemurs.

A lemur's life cycle

Lemurs begin mating when they are two to three years old. They have one mating season a year, usually during April. It lasts for about two weeks.

In many lemur species, the females will choose their mates. In other species, it is the males that choose the females. Male lemurs often fight with each other if they both want to mate with the same female. They may scratch and bite each other. The winner of the fight gets to mate with the female.

After mating, the female gives birth. Most females give birth to only one or two young lemurs at a time. But ruffed lemurs have more than two young. Females of these species give birth to as many as six young lemurs at a time.

Young lemurs

Females sometimes carry their young around in their mouths. But most newborn lemurs have a strong grip. They spend their first few weeks holding on to the fur on their mother's stomach. Young lemurs drink milk from their mother's body. This is called **nursing**.

Because ruffed lemurs have so many young at a time, they do not carry them around. Instead, the mother makes a nest of leaves and twigs. She leaves her young in the nest while she looks for food.

After three weeks, a young lemur is strong enough to hold on to its mother's back. It also begins to take its first steps. It does not walk far, and comes back to ride on its mother's back. In some species, a young lemur will ride on its father's back, too.

During the next four to five months, a young lemur still rides on its mother's or father's back. But it leaves its parents for longer periods of time. It begins to eat solid foods and drinks less of its mother's milk.

After five or six months, a young lemur stops drinking its mother's milk. Then it begins to

▲ **This young sifaka is old enough to ride on its mother's back.**

travel with the group on its own. After two or three years, it is fully grown.

Fully grown males leave the groups where they were born. They join other groups or find a home range and start new groups. Females stay in the groups in which they were born.

Some species of lemurs live for 15 to 20 years. Others live for up to 30 years or more.

 You can see the dental comb in this red-bellied lemur's lower jaw.

Surviving in the rainforest

Lemurs are in danger from **predators**. A predator is an animal that hunts and eats other animals. Eagles, snakes, hawks and fossa will eat lemurs. Fossa are weasel-like animals that live only in Madagascar.

To keep safe, lemurs call out to warn other lemurs of danger. Some species have a special warning call for each kind of predator. Scientists think the warning call tells other lemurs whether the predator is in the air or on the ground.

The larger species of lemur are active during the day. They get up in the morning and look for food and water. They spend several hours searching for food and eating.

Around the middle of the day, the lemurs take a break. They rest in the trees or groom each other. Grooming is when the lemurs help clean each other. The grooming time helps them get to know the other members of their group.

A lemur uses its teeth to help it groom. A lemur's six lower middle teeth point outwards instead of upwards and have small spaces between them. These teeth are known as the dental comb. The lemur uses this dental comb to brush its fur and other lemurs' fur.

Smaller lemurs that are active at night do many of the same things as lemurs that are active during the day. But they sleep during the day and search for food at night. This way, the small lemurs do not have to fight with the big lemurs for food. It is also easier for them to hide from predators at night.

The fat-tailed dwarf lemur eats mainly fruit, flowers and occasionally insects.

The future of lemurs

Until about 2000 years ago, Madagascar was completely wild. No people lived there. Then the first people arrived on the island and began to live there. They cleared away forests and grew their own food. After a while, they built towns and cities. Today, about 16.5 million people live on Madagascar.

When people first came to Madagascar, there were about 50 different species of lemur. The largest lemur was nearly the size of a gorilla. Other lemur species hung upside down from trees. Sadly, these lemur species have become **extinct**. Extinct means that no animals of that species are left in the wild.

Now there are only about 36 different species of lemur left. Most of these species are in danger of becoming extinct.

▲ At 2.25 kilograms, the aye-aye is the largest nocturnal primate in the world.

What will happen to lemurs?

Lemurs are in danger because some people hunt them as food. People also cut down trees to make farmland and to build houses. Fires burn parts of the rainforest. Today, only 10 per cent of the Madagascar rainforest is left. Without the trees to live in and provide food, lemurs will die.

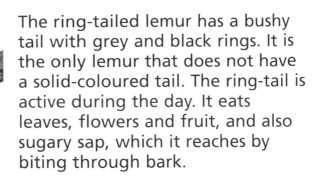

The ring-tailed lemur has a bushy tail with grey and black rings. It is the only lemur that does not have a solid-coloured tail. The ring-tail is active during the day. It eats leaves, flowers and fruit, and also sugary sap, which it reaches by biting through bark.

People now know that lemurs are important to the health of the rainforest. Some of the seeds from the fruits they eat leave their bodies as waste. Waste is what the body does not use from food. Lemurs spread the seeds as they move through the forest. New plants grow from the seeds.

Some people are working to save lemurs. To do this, they have set up reserves in some areas of Madagascar. It is against the law to cut down trees or build in these reserves.

Some scientists are raising lemurs in zoos. When these lemurs are older, scientists may release some of them into the wild. Scientists also keep some lemurs to study.

By stopping hunters and saving the rainforest, scientists hope to keep lemurs alive in their homes for a long time to come.

head
see page 10

eyes
see pages 11, 12

ruff
see pages 10, 11

long, fox-like nose
see pages 7, 11

fur
see page 10

long tail
see page 10

Glossary

arboreal living mainly in trees

bamboo tree-like grass with a woody stem

binocular vision using both eyes at the same time to help focus

canopy (KAN-uh-pee) thick area of leaves high up in the treetops

extinct when a species of animal or plant has disappeared forever

groom to clean – an animal may groom itself or other animals in its group

nocturnal active at night

nursing when a mother feeds her young milk made inside her body

omnivore animal that eats both plants and animals

predator animal that hunts other animals

primate mammal that has a large brain and hands that can grasp and hold objects

species group of animals or plants most closely related to each other

warm-blooded animals that stay at a steady warm temperature

Internet sites

Madagascar Fauna Group
www.SaveTheLemur.org

World Wide Fund for Nature
www.panda.org

Useful address

World Wildlife Fund-UK
Panda House, Weyside Park
Godalming, Surrey
GU7 1XR

Books to read

Theodorou, R; Telford, C. *Amazing journeys: Up a Rainforest Tree.* Heinemann Library, Oxford, 1998

Index